Kingdom Magick

By <u>Elijah Autumn</u>

All Quotes and phrases that are found between the chapters are written solely by the author, *Elijah Autumn.*

All Scripture references in this book come from one of two versions of the Holy Bible.

1.)King James Version (KJV)
2.)New International version (NIV)

ISBN #13: 978-0615888057
ISBN# 10: 0615888054

Table of Contents

Introduction

Thank you for your purchase of
Kingdom Magick.

The book you are about to read, is the
first of what will be many more books to
come. The ideas and practices within
this book hope to ignite a new move of
the spirit. By empowering and
enlightening believers worldwide with
the wisdom and understanding of what
the kingdom of God actually is, and
what it means.

It is written in an easy to read and
understand format that is aimed to all
people, whether they be a spiritual
novice, (beginner) or a seasoned
person of faith.

Kingdom magick is for those

individuals that believe that both magick and miracles are indeed real. It is for all Christians that have found themselves drawn to spiritual practices such as Wicca or witchcraft, due to either the complacency or rebellious division found, within the modern day church. Or, it is simply that they desire a more interactive and personal experience, then what they have previously found in their local church setting.

These people understand and believe in real spiritual power. Yet, have only witnessed what seems to be nothing but a powerless and hateful body of confused believers, in many of the churches worldwide. They desire to sit under the spirit of truth and love, yet have had a difficult time finding it in the local church memberships.

Kingdom Magick isn't just for the searching Christian however, it is also for those individuals that have already explored the practices that may hold to these magickal overtones, and yet are still powerfully drawn to the Christian practice and theology. Some may want to place a term on Kingdom magick such as Christian Wicca, or a similar term, but I believe it stands on its own.

Before you truly dive into this book, please note that the aim of this book is *NOT* to teach the practice of what many may term as the stereotyped version of witchcraft. Rather, the goal is to simply express and teach the fundamental fact, that magick in itself, is neither good nor evil. The differences begin from within the individual. Practicing Magick can be so easily seen as the same as the performance of miracles.

The truth of the matter is, the center of both magick and miracle, comes from within us, and is simply what it is. It is the manifestation of our spiritual self, forcing change in our physical world just as Jesus said we could. Practitioners of Kingdom magick are merely the light workers of the world.

Think spiritual power is just illusion,
fables, or just old time stories? Perhaps
people have told you that it's just power
hungry people that search for it? Let's
examine the scripture found in 1st
Corinthians 4:20.

*"For the kingdom of God is not a matter
of talk, but of power"* (NIV)

Do you have power in your faith? Do
you see power in those around you?
These are questions to really consider
for true seeker of truth.

It is in my deepest convictions that I
hold to the wisdom, that Kingdom
magick does not fall under the same
terminology or category as what many
may term as witchcraft, or sorcery. Yes,
many of the practices and beliefs may
be closely alike in appearance, but the
differences I believe, lie from within
each person and to their individual
character.

We can compare that thought to the scripture in the book of Mark, chapter seven. In verse 20 it reads,

"What comes out of you is what defiles you."

In many ways we are all brothers in sisters in the magickal arena, but differences do exist. Much like each child has their own personality and desires, each practice has its own traditions and moral concepts. Respect is given to all however. We all learn from each other.

Such differences in terminology can be measured in both intention, and moral character of the practitioner. It is also measured upon who, or what, a practitioner chooses within themselves to serve or worship. It can also be measured upon the choice of not serving or worshiping anything, if that be the case. It can be measured by varying theology, and individual beliefs. Terms or labels can be so stereotyped

and misleading when it comes to faith
or religion.

None of us are the same, and the
Divine may have one way of teaching
one person, and yet another way for
someone else. The basic truth is
always the same, but the paths to that
truth, may not be walked by all people
at the same time.

To simplify it means, that to use
Kingdom magick, is to use the same
manifested power used by those in
both the Old Testament, and in the New
Testament. This power is also seen
today, in many of the real miracles we
have seen and heard about throughout
the world. It is the same power that
dwells with you right now as you read
this book.

Jesus of Nazareth, and each and
every one of the Prophets documented
in written text, used the basic concepts
that will be described in this book. It is
applied to all those individuals from

which miracles have been documented throughout the written word, and that have been called - *Men and women of God.*

This book is the first to be released to the public by the author, and is sure to meet with some opposition. It is the conviction of the author however, to help bring to light a truth that has been cunningly hidden and suppressed by even the modern day Christian church as a whole. Whether to point to whether it is intentional or unintentional is not the goal at this point, but it is simply to reveal the truth today as it is in its completion.

It is stand against all those allowing the confinement of the people by allowing the teaching of partial truth, and of the rigged enforcement of suppressing laws that are preached only for the benefit of group control, and for the personal gain of those seeking power and control over the people. The real Jesus taught about freedom and spiritual liberty. He taught about the Kingdom of God and of the gift within all of us. That gift was to have victory over our own lives.

Kingdom Magick will help put your faith, with real practice. It will enhance your faith into real action. It mixes some of the same principals and rituals that a person might find in the earth based religion known as Wicca. You will also find elements of other magickal believing practices within it as well. This is done because it is my opinion that there is truth to found in many faiths and practices. As seekers we are not bias or against any positive faith, but take from each one, truth, for what it is.

Kingdom Magick chooses to utilize ceremonial and ritual tools, much like that found in practices containing magickal overtones, yet it should not to be confused as being one in the same however. It is separate and set apart from all others. Although in Kingdom magick we utilize these tools to help us, please note that such tools are not mandatory for all spiritual development. Many of us simply prefer to use them because they aid in us in developing our focus and healthy spiritual discipline.

Kingdom Magick's, creed of ethics is based on these main areas of teaching, but are not solely limited to simply this list.

1.) *Scripture (Christian and other faiths)*
2.) *Prophetic writings (old and new)*
3.) *Current and past spirit inspired works*
4.) *Principals found within the earth based religion known as Wicca,*
5.) *Wiccan Rede*
6) *Life of Jesus Christ*

Please remember Kingdom magick is not Wicca, but it only contains many of the same elements that one will find within it. Its foundation is built upon a loving Creator and the discovery of complete truth. As you grow and study, you will begin to notice similarities and common wordings that relate together into the same common truth.

I understand that many will be hesitate to understand how these practices can mix without theological conflict, but please continue to read, and your answer, will soon become clear.

Above all things, Kingdom Magick is a spirit led practice that requires a deep devotion to the study of truth and a clear intention. It requires a person of both integrity and honor. It requires a person that is not easily bought out by the persuasion of evil practices and unmoral standards. It seeks to help people become all that the creator wishes them to be, and all that Jesus said they can be.

Practitioners of Kingdom magick are simply those people that hear the gentle voice of the spirit. They are those individuals that understand more naturally, the spiritual and magickal side of life. These individuals many times, tend to possess a magical quality within the life they live, and have been drawn to such things since their birth. They are called to it, because it is what they were born to do.

Many will remark to you on your journey, that to live a life practicing any kind of magickal practice, simply defines you as somewhat of a witch. To a degree, that is true. Yet, only in the sense that we do believe we can control, and mold many of the things in our own lives using a manifested power. We believe this because Jesus said we can, and as practitioners we do not wish to forsake the power that we all have been instructed we hold within.

It is my sincere opinion to consider simply laying down descriptive labels for now, and simply rely on the spirit to guild you, and to teach you as you read and research the things the spirit leads you to.

This book is the first to go print on this particular subject presented as such by the author. Please remember it is only a basic layout of the idea of Kingdom Magick, and many more will come and with the spirit's help, and with much greater detail.

Congratulations on the beginning of a journey that will be filled with magickal blessings and spiritual connections.

Get ready, to discover the true magick within you.

"Be led by the spirit and not the ranting shouts of carnal religionist"

The Authors thoughts

As the wind blows, it carries with it the ancient voices of all those that have pasted before us. Nature's magnificent beauty has been carved out by a loving creator that resides in everything we see, and within the very essence of what, and who we are as individuals.

Truth is indeed real, and it can be heard on the tailwind of the distant breeze. It rustles through the many trees, and speaks somewhere within the heart of each of us, that are open to its voice.

It is the spirit that speaks so softy within the wind. It carries with it, a truth that completes us, and grants us a real spiritual freedom, that I believe we all look for in our lives.

Jesus the Christ said this:

The Kingdom of God is within you.
(Luke 17:21)

Kingdom magick is what I call the
manifested magick, which comes from
this inward Kingdom that Jesus spoke
of. From it, can flow fountains of love
and manifested power that most
modern religions today, either have no
concept of, or that simply refuse to
teach it due to persecution, ridicule or
even fear itself.

People often fear the things that they
don't understand. Many more times
they have simply been brainwashed
into thinking one bias and unwavering
way or another. People have lost their
connection with real divinity period.
Whether it is due to fear, or simply an
apathetic attitude towards real
spirituality, I suppose lies the answer to
why. Perhaps, many have simply
conformed to what the mainstream idea
of what faith should look like, and to
how a person should think and act and

have forgotten the act of searching or seeking, as the spirit tells us to do?

The kingdom of God and all that is spiritual, springs forth from the center of our being and is brought to life by the spirit of love and an a open mind towards real truth. The ability to listen to something outside of the everyday chaos of humanity is a key factor in receiving any revelation of truth from the spirit.

I believe truth isn't found in any specific religion by itself, and it most definitely isn't solely found in any physical building or in a denominational title, but it lies quietly within each of us and in the works and writings of those scattered around the globe in many practicing faiths. It is the individuals that are led by the spirit that find the scattered puzzle pieces and learn to apply them together to accurately discover one real universal truth.

Within us all, lies the power of God.

Yes, it may be the size of a mustard seed, and it may even be completely dormant. But through the willingness to listen, and to accept the teachings of the spirit, we can harness all that the Divine one wishes for us in our lives. We can have the power to gain victory over many of life's challenges, which are thrown our way.

We are all children of the divine creator, and within each of us resides the power to do miracles and magick.

That is right, I said - *magick*.

Many of us have read about miracles and magickal events. We have seen or felt them in the rituals or ceremonies we have practiced in our lives whether we are Christian, Pagan or any other faith.

It is this magick I speak of that shines forth from the inner kingdom that like the title of the book reads, I call - *Kingdom Magick*.

As said before, though resembling it,
Kingdom magick isn't witchcraft as
many may use the term, but it is more
of a God craft than anything else. It is
the power that always was, is and that
will continue on to be. It has been the
same from the very beginning.

Man derived terminology, and one's
individual preference are the only
things in my opinion that truly separates
the term's meanings. Just as one
symbol, can hold many meanings from
many branches of religion, so can a
word, have many preconceived and
bias definitions.

Regardless of the terminology, the
power within each us is real, and it is
the basis of where all truth and spiritual
revelation begin. It is the topic of this
book you hold in your hand.

Though there may be many paths
among each of our separate journeys,

there is but one real truth. This truth does not hide its face from us. Rather, it is us that most often choose to ignore the forces that call out to us each day and that cry out within us, day after day, to simply acknowledge this truth without turning in doubt. Often the truth isn't as difficult as people believe it to be. Most often it's simply that their running so hard after preconceived ideas or mindsets that they pass by the very thing that they were searching for.

Mankind in its fleshly attempt to create some sort of spiritual and physical harmony without accepting the intervention of spirit, has in my opinion simply created a powerless and divided body of blind believers throughout the world, and it is one that only confuses those wanting real truth.

I believe, that many of the people in our world, that make claims to be true spiritual seekers ,have either become unable to listen to the spirit's voice due to life's unending chaos, or have simply

chosen not to accept within
themselves, the voice that is kindred to
that which has been carried as a
whisper on nature's own cries.

They deny their own convictions, and
to the pulling of the spirit itself, and they
have done so since creation first
began.

"One man firm in the declaration of truth far outweighs a hundred men willing to compromise it. "

Us and the elements

Starting now, we need to empty ourselves of all our preconceived ideas, and learn to listen to the mother of which we were all originally created from. We need to focus our attention on the spirit, (The Divine) that rides on her mighty winds, and offers guidance through such a desolate auditorium of theological turmoil and emptiness. Let me explain because this is a major key factor in our ability to completely understand the answers to life's most difficult questions.

We are all, of the earth itself. One could even say that she is our mother. Yes, we all do have a physical biological mother, but Mother nature could be said to be the mother of all mothers. From her (the earth) , all physical life was created here on this planet.

The Christian Bible teaches us that the Divine (God) took from the dirt of the earth, and from the elements, created our physical bodies. The elements of Mother Nature reside in each of us, and when we die, those elements are thus again returned to her. Everything we are physically, originates from Mother Earth.

If we apply that fact for example within just one area within the magickal arena, such as crystals and precious stones, we could easily see a real correlation on how they might just physically and mentally really affect us. After all, they are consistent of the same properties that our bodies are made up of, correct?

It is for this reason; that I do believe that many stones, gems, and beautiful crystals, can indeed have a real effect on us, as mortal and physical beings. I believe there is both a real magical and a scientific reason if you will, to the cause and effect that they may have on each of us. Why – very Simple. It is because we are, of the same essence or properties that they are.

The main principal ideas are simply that our physical bodies do indeed originate from the essence of the earth and thus, I and many others choose to call her mother. We hold to the fact that other external elements can and do have positive or negative effects on our physical self. I will go into this in more detail at a later time.

Our spiritual Father and Mother Nature combined have created what is our soul. A soul is made up of a physical body and a spirit. Everything we see in Mother Nature is alive and breathing. Though there is death, we see how life regenerates itself, and how it continues on, don't we? In this, we can see that Mother Nature is far more than simply dirt and rock, but I believe she is alive, and it is our duty to care for her, just as she tends to us. Everything that grows and sustains itself has life within it, even if that life is not like that of our likeness.

Caring for the earth is backed by scriptural, to be mankind's responsibility. As it reads, that we were created to rule over it. We can read it in Genesis 1:26. It reads as such,

"Then God said, "Let us make mankind in our image, in our likeness so that they may rule over the fish in the sea and the birds in the sky, over the livestock and all the wild animals, and over all the creatures that move along the ground."

In Kingdom magick we should honor the Divine and do our best to take care of mother earth and to harm none. Just as is seen in Wicca and other magickal beliefs. In doing so, nothing but good things can come forth from it.

"Finding complete truth is much like completing a circle. Many people may start at different locations within the circle, with none being the standard beginning or end, but simply the beginning for each individual. We must complete the circle. Open your mind and discover what lies just around the bend."

Miracles and Magick

I believe, what defines things as being evil, flows from the hearts and minds of the people. It is a matter of personal character or integrity that defines. It is from this vanity and corruption, which springs out negative and destructive energies that cause so much fear and confusion towards the subject of manifested power and magick. Magick however is merely a term, and how we apply that term is what truly defines it as good or evil.

Kingdom Magick teaches that both miracles and magick are one in the same. When speaking of these terms, I am referring to the essence of the power in itself. The terms are neither evil, nor are they simply good, but only become one or the another from the directed energy that flows from the heart of the practicing individual, or simply put, in the direct intention of the one engaged in it.

Throughout history we can read about documented miracles in religious texts, and if we compare them to the term of Magick, we will realize that they are two words, that can very easily work simultaneously together and effectively be one, with one real meaning.

There have been both good and bad men throughout history that can be found in many different religious text. Many of these men had performed what can be termed as doing magick or preforming a miracle. It was simply a matter of faith, or their personal belief, that measured just how each occurrence could be applied. Regardless however, the power itself was neither good nor bad but what would define it would simply be in the individual themselves. Both Magick and miracles are simply defined as the directed intention of will to remold a given situation. Such events have been documented throughout history.

On record we read that Jesus himself changed the water into wine. He caused the death of the fig tree, and he raised a man from death. He healed many of the sicknesses in his time.

Was it simply because of his spiritual divinity? Or could it have been that he just understood his inward potential, and how to harness the essence of this kingdom within himself? What it means is, he truly understood the reality of the stored up manifested power within himself, by simply being a child of God. This is not taking from Jesus, any of his divinity, but examines the idea that it wasn't his divinity that granted him manifested power but that it was merely his knowledge and understanding of the Kingdom of God that is in all of us at birth that enabled him.

Now I ask this question. If, we are all children of God, as the Bible tells us that we are, then can each of us harness this same kingdom power, just as Jesus did? Remember, that Jesus was quoted as saying this.

"Greater things will you do, than I". (John 14:12)

We have to also remember that the religious leaders in Jesus's time were absolutely sure that he was a heretic, and full of vain evil intentions. They proclaimed that the miracles that he performed were from that of an evil source or intention. Today however, we can understand that was not the case at all, but it was merely their misinterpretation of scripture, and bias ignorance of the real facts as the Divine had spoken them before.

If we read we will find that miracles are not solely found in Jesus's life either. They were found in many of the old prophets of the Old Testament, and also in many other religious texts throughout the world as well.

Everything, from healing the sick to resurrection can be found if we simply take the time to look. The Old Testament is full of magickal happenings that can be easily associated with miracles. Look at these examples below. Take some time and read them, examine how things such as Moses and his staff were used, or how he used it. Examine how the staff and the wand are used closely in the same. Way. (Examples 1 &4)

1.)*Moses and the Red sea.* (Exodus 14:26)

2.)*Elijah and the prophets of Baal* (1Kings 18:16)

3.)*Elijah stops the rain* (1 Kings 17)

4.)*Moses staff becomes a snake* (Exodus 17:10)

5.)*Elisha resurrects dead son of Shunamite* (2 Kings 4:33)

If we look, we will find that In many religions we will uncover many ceremonies that resemble the same likeness of those coming from say Wicca, or any other faith with magickal undertones. Though I do believe each ceremony can be different according to its tradition and formed intention. The manifested power used, still branches from the same roots or origin. It is what is inside us and that is projected that makes all the difference.

Note: This is based upon the notion that the power we are using is within us, and not that we are attempting to use other spiritual forces besides that of ourselves. In Kingdom magick, we are the one in control. We are submissive to the teaching of the spirit, although we also fully understand the biblical teaching found in 1 Corinthians 14:32, when it reads,

"The Spirit of the prophets are subject

to the control of the prophets."

Key words here are, the spirit of the prophets (or practitioner) being under control of the prophet, and not the spirit controlling the prophet. (Or practitioner)

Let's look at one example of a similarity found in both magickal and spiritual ceremonies. Incense for example, is used in many types of magickal and spiritual ceremonies. It is seen largely in the Old Testament and in a huge amount of religious text all over the world. It has been used for centuries by many faiths and practitioners of all sorts. One example can be found in Exodus 30:7.

"Aaron must burn fragrant incense on the alter every morning when he tends the lamps." (NIV)

Kingdom Magick is based on the concept that miracles and magick are one in the same. The only differences dwell within us, and in our directed intentions. I suppose one could say, that would be were the meat would be then, wouldn't it? Who are we inside? Do we serve vain or arrogant intentions or selfless and honorable? Do we seek peace, or are we full of hate, and run after war? Do we seek to use dark or evil spirits as guilds, or do we choose rather to use those that honored the Divine and followed in the spirit of love. These are the things that separate the differences in practice and definition.

Kingdom magick teaches that magick in itself is neither evil, nor is it wrong. It teaches that the origin of both magick and miracles start within each of us. It holds to the belief that the essence of both, are of the same manifested power that Jesus, and all others on record and off , used in their documented miraculous events throughout time. It is the same power used by any practicing wiccan, witch, sorcerer or spell caster - or Christian today, excluding those that practice the arts of demonology and similar dark practices. If you don't know the difference please take some time and study them before you proceed.

 In Kingdom Magick, we teach that we do acknowledge the presence or existence of what many term as gods and goddesses, just as many in the Christian church, recognize past saints. We do NOT however worship all gods, nor do we serve them, just as the churches such as the Catholic Church, will not worship or serve their saints. We understand that the Bible and other religious text do in fact give evidence that they exist in reality. We can view a small dose of evidence of this in Psalms 82; 6, 7) it reads,

"I said you are gods, and all of you are children of the Most High. "

Some will say that to believe in any other God or Goddess, or to pray to a past saint is sin or evil in the modern sense of the word, but truth is truth, and truth is what it is.

The Old Testament law states in
Exodus 20:3,

*You shall have no other gods before
me*"

We can look at that in two ways we can
look at it from the point of view that the
Divine one wishes no other god's be in
his physical sight, or we can view it as it
truly reads. The scripture reads that the
Divine commands that no other little '
g"' god be placed before him. Could this
be seen much like a list of priorities or
say a list of top governing officials?
Each official has their own rank in
importance or command. Is the Divine
simply reminding us to take care to
always hold him first above all things?

We are the followers of the real Jesus
of Nazareth, and believe that there is
far more to learn from Jesus, and his
life, then what the modern church
teaches us. We believe that though the
original writings within the Bible are
indeed inspired, we also believe, that

through the years, mankind has corrupted many of the original meanings and or terminologies. This in turn has caused the growth of a somewhat powerless and divided modern day church. It is one that is lacking of its fullest potential. Kingdom magick means to restore the spiritual power in believers once again.

 Some will still try to tell you that magick in itself is purely evil, and that scripture strictly forbids any form of witchcraft, sorcery or use of magick. Though it does mention in the Old Testament to stay away from practices relating to these stereotyped terms, what we have to consider is the context and application in which the terms are applied, and if that term still applies to what we are practicing ourselves. I believe that as I said earlier, many of the issues come from improper terminology or stereotyping.

 Ask yourself this question, what physically manifested power do you think Jesus and the prophets used when they performed all of their miracles? No one can dispute that the term miracle can come pretty close to the same appearance and definition as found in the term magick. Both terms are equally the physically manifested execution of an inward power.

What better way to confine a world or a group of people, then to convince them that the victorious power within them is evil? What better way to leave them powerless than to convince them that to use the gift within them, would surely be punishable by eternal torment?

We also need to remember that the 66 books that make up the Christian Bible are only a fraction of the spirit inspired writings that have been written over time.

It was in 325 AD that Constantine the Great called the first Council of Nicaea. The council was composed of 300 religious leaders. Take in mind this was three centuries after Jesus lived. During this time the divinity of Jesus had split the church already into two fractions and Constantine had offered to make the Christian sect the official state religion if they could simply settle their differences. This council was filled with dissension, jealousy, intolerance, persecution and bigotry.

During this time the council would debate and divide the many writings into those that would go into the corporate Bible and those that would be left out. Many people believe today that only these selected 66 books are considered scripture, but my friends, that is anything but truth. Even the Bible says this about the subject.

"All Scripture is God breathed and is useful for teaching, rebuking, correcting and training in righteousness." (2 Timothy 3:16)

Scripture is any written word that has been inspired or God breathed by the

Divine. Could the decision of the Council to limit the Bible to these sixty six books have also created the faith that we see today. It is divided and powerless. Could that be because we know in our spirit that there is so much more to Christianity then what we see in the modern church?

But we are taught by tradition that to read anything else is sin, are we not? I'm here to tell you that without reading other inspired words we limit our knowledge and wisdom to only a fraction of our fullest potential.

I want to give one example that I feel speaks loudly on this issue. The book of Enoch, except for a very few churches, is said to be unworthy of study. Yet in Genesis 5:24 we read.

"And Enoch walked with God; and he was not, for God took him"

I ask this one question. If Enoch was a man that walked with God, why would the church refuse to teach of him or his words? It was because Enoch wrote of things, much like what you are reading on right now.

Please do not think that I do not discredit the Bible, how could I? It is used it daily in Kingdom magick, What I am saying is, that I don't believe we can be all that the Divine wants us to be, if we limit ourselves to the reading of only one book that only contains perhaps half the proper information needed to interpret truth clearly. Do to this, I personally feel we need a wider viewpoint on the whole subject, and can only achieve that by allowing ourselves to read all the information available to us. Through the years words can become blurred or misinterpreted, but if we read enough, we can with the spirit's help, separate truth from fiction, and put together real truth from such a scattered mess of lies and deceit.

The Council debated even the divinity

of Jesus. But when we speak about Jesus we need to remember one thing. In order to be the sacrifice that was needed to cleanse mankind of its sin, Jesus had to be fully human in his flesh. He had to fully possess all the crazy human emotions and temptations we all face each and every day on earth and in our daily lives.

 Since this is the case. Jesus had to have learned how to harness the power within the kingdom that is described in the bible itself, and by his own words. He had to have been taught and trained to use it. This universal power is the same power Jesus describes that we all possess if we merely believe.

 Just as Peter (a disciple of Christ) walked on water for a brief moment before doubt and fear sank him. (Matthew 14:29) He had within himself the same power as Jesus did to walk on that same water. I ask you, was that evil? No, it wasn't, not in the slightest. Universal magick is the essence and reality of spiritual power in a spiritual realm and one that Jesus said and showed was also in the physical.

There is a basic phrase used in Wicca and other religions of the sort, which root from Hermeticism or from the writer Hermes Trimegistus. It reads:

"As above, so below".

In the Bible it reads slightly different but with the same meaning. It reads:

"Truly I tell you, whatever you bind on earth will be bound in Heaven, and whatever you, loose on earth, will be loosed in Heaven". (Matthew 18:18)

In layman's terms, what you release in the spiritual realm, will affect the physical.

The modern day church has lost its concept of spiritual power. The corruption of half teaching and the lack of searching for truth, has built a spiritually and physically divided weak version of what Jesus intended as his church.

A new fellowship, of believers is forming however, and it will be a united one. It will be one that understands the true potential in all people, and one that believes that they too can reach past the normal barriers of plain human existence. They just need to learn how to tap into that power just as the others did. Kingdom magick hopes to help to do that.

Kingdom Magick is for those individuals that believe in the same power that we read about in the life of Jesus, the prophets, and other miracle or magickal working people. It is also for those that desire knowledge of God's true nature, and that choose to work towards real truth and spiritual freedom.

To do this, I would advise all of my readers, to read and research daily, the many divinely inspired words that fill our libraries and internet. I urge you to read the Bible an take from it, a knowledge of God's nature and to the documents events that have taken place throughout time. But, don't stop there, take the time to also read the words of other seekers, for in them are pieces of the scattered puzzle that make up the truth.

Do not forsake, or push aside any spiritual work, but rather, try to compare what you have read to the confirmation of the spirit and to the other authors you have learned from. Remember, it is the spirit that will lead you into real truth. The spirit will help you divide the real truth from that of fiction. Don't be afraid to explore and to challenge what you read.

Use your daily walk to learn. Watch and listen to people, and to what the spirit says about them. Do not judge them, but simply learn from them.

Look into Mother Nature. Stop the chaos of life, and for just a moment, gaze into the beauty of her majesty. The things you will see are far beyond amazing, if you will truly open your mind and heart to her voice.

Let the whispers on the winds speak to you. Every creature that has breath shines the radiant truth of the purpose of life, and gives evidence of loving creator.

"A calm word of wisdom far outweighs many vain words of emotion any day. Listen to the voice of reason, and your path will meet up with many less thorny bushes on the way".

Using Kingdom Magick

Kingdom magick is simply using the magick or power found within the Kingdom of God. That Kingdom as described earlier is found within each and every one of us. It is the God given gift received by every individual upon birth as a child of God.

As in other practices, a person may alter their specific manner of practice slightly different than others, but a basic standard of ethics must be applied to all that function with the Kingdom magick principals. I would recommend a basic background in some kind of religious studies and a devotion to the continued study of all religions. More books will follow.

In Kingdom magick we pray in the same manner as Jesus of Nazareth taught. In this manner, we take all requests to the Father. We ask aid of the angels or spirits as we work in our practice. To us, the terms of prayers and spells are both one in the same, just as miracles and magick. We believe there are rules and that there are things we may ask of, and there are things that we should not. Just as God (the Divine) will not move against a person's free will, neither should we move to cast spells against that free will either.

As described earlier, we recognize the presence of the spiritual realm, and that these spirits or angels, which ever term if you prefer, will help guild us and protect us. We can find even specific names to certain high ranking angels within the text of the Holy Bible and other writings such as the Dead Sea scrolls. NOTE: We do not worship spirits or angels, but in practice we only ask them help with from them for guidance and understanding.

Start small. Take your time and get

comfortable in your practice. Write down what you do, and how each time was different or better than the last. Learn what things work for you, because with each person will come varying approaches and techniques.

Remember Kingdom magick is based on the spirit of love and temperance, never hate or anger. A solid standard of moral practice needs to be seen in all of our practices. We seek to live and work in harmony with everyone regardless of race, religion, sex, or even sexual preference.

We do not condemn, but only love, and leave the judging of the soul of another strictly to the Divine one's control.

"Destiny isn't discovered by the simple exploration of worldly experiences, but it is simply found, when we learn to search within ourselves, and to accept what has always been within us."

Basic rituals and tools

In this book you will find many rituals and or ceremonies used to help focus an individual's intention, or will. What we must understand however is that the power is not in the rituals or in the ceremony, but it is within us.

Rituals and ceremonies simply help us to combat the chaos surrounding us, and to increase our ability to focus. We use tools of the craft to aim our projected thoughts and prayers, and to deliver them with greater force and impact.

Whether a person chooses to call them spells or prayers, is simply a matter of what again? That's right - simple terminology.

The essence of what they are is purely a manifestation of Spiritual energy used to mold physical matter or cause change in a physical or spiritual presence. It is only becomes evil, if the individual themselves, has evil intentions and directs that evil, in an effort to do harm against an unwilling individual's person or will.

To understand God's (the Divine) nature we must understand the Divine's essence. The Bible says God is a spirit, and is love. But what is love? Let's look at what the Bible says about love. It reads,

"Love *is patient, Love is kind, it does not envy, it does not boast, it is not proud. It does not dishonor others, it is not self-seeking",* it is not easily *angered; it keeps no record of wrongs. Love does not delight in evil but rejoices with the truth. (1* Corinthians 13:4)

With this knowledge of love, we can better understand within ourselves, if what we are doing lines up with the spirit of love. We can better aim our intentions to center on this love, and to avoid both what the Wiccan rede rule of three say, and to what the Biblical statement of "what *you sow, so shall you reap*".

The rule of three states that,

What energy you send out, will return to you three fold (karma).

We then can also compare that, to the scripture found in Galatians 6:7 which declares,

"Be not deceived, God is not mocked, whatever a man sows that shall he also reap." (KJV)

Now, with that said, we understand that there are real consequences to our actions. When using any magick, even Kingdom magick, we must make sure that our intentions are clear and pure. Before casting any spell or prayer ask the spirit for understanding. Never use the power of the Kingdom of God to attempt to do wrong. It will surely come back to haunt you.

 Let's talk about some the tools a person practicing Kingdom magick could use in the development of their everyday practice.

As you grow and build upon your own practice, you will most likely create and use different tools, and you will learn to apply your own methods. Not all of these tools must be used and not everyone's exact method needs to be the same. As you grow remember to write down what you did, so that you can repeat it in the same manner. What works good for one, may not work so well for another. We are all different.

Here are simply a few listed tools that may be used:

1.) Crystals and stones
2.) Herbs and plants
3.) Candles

4.) Incense
5.) Athame or dagger
6.) Wand or staff
7.)spells or prayer book

 With each tool, comes a different purpose. Crystals and stones help to create change, or empowerment by utilizing the individual energies found with each one. Each crystal or stone carries with it a different energy. Crystals and stones must be cleansed and charged before used in our rituals or practices. I will speak on this in a throughout the book and in a later chapter.

 Herbs and plants obviously are used in medicines or potions, depending on your preferred terminology.

 Used correctly, these herbs and various edible plants can work to heal sicknesses and can even empower us. They can boost our immune system, give us greater energy levels, or even completely heal us. They can even create a calming sensation, or a tranquil attitude in a normally stressed environment.

I would advise however, that a person take some time and study before offering their potions and herbal medicines to the public. Remember, It is illegal to practice medicine without a license. No one wants to the see anyone get hurt, not including what the legal aspects of it would be if things were to go wrong. Be cautious and professional.

Candles are one of the most widely used tools. We see them in almost every tradition and religion. You probably have noticed them in everything from Catholic ceremonies, Wiccan Rituals and even aroma therapy applications.

Even the people that do not practice, still use the candle, to create an atmosphere of aroma that is pleasing to their guest and family, and to somewhat control the environment with calming scents do they not?

Without realizing it, I believe, we can go as far to say that in a roundabout way, these people still do practice without necessarily even thinking about it.

Candles are much more than just their scents however, they all have various colors, and each color represents something different and corresponds with the directed intention of the spell or prayer. Depending on the desired outcome, a different color candle should be used. There are many books on the market that will examine this. I will go deeper into this as well later.

Incense has been used for centuries and dates back to biblical times and possibly even before. They used it in their ceremonies and rituals and is documented throughout the Bible, and in recorded text of many other religions as well.

Incense, is not only used for creating an atmosphere, much like the candle, but it is used to also cleanse it. The sweeping of burning incense, pushes out the negative energies stagnated in a given space, and clears it so it can be filled with pure and positive energy. It can also be used to cleanse our crystals and our stones before we charge them with directed positive energy.

An Athame uses a double edged blade, and most often is seen with a black handle. It is used predominantly in Wicca, but is also used in other practices including witchcraft itself. It is symbolic of the element of fire, but can also be seen as air, depending on the particular practice.

It is a largely use ritual tool in many practices, but is not used for actual cutting. Depending on your particular tailored craft-style the Athame made be used in different ways. I may go in deeper detail at a later time with this as well.

The wand or staff is a tool used to aim our intention. Many people create their own homemade wands or staff. I personally like to use crystals and various stones on a wand. The crystal amplifies the intention, and in my opinion can direct it with much greater force and impact.

What we always have to remember is that manifested power isn't in the tool, but it comes from within the Kingdom. Far too many people get carried away with the tools of the trade and lose focus on developing the true center of the power - us.

Our spell books or prayer books, often called the book of shadows or journals are the heart of our rituals and ceremonies. The words within the text of each spell or prayer are the directing force of our intention or personal will.

The written word is indeed powerful but the spoken word causes real change and physical re-shifting if pronounced with faith and determination. Even Jesus said in Mark 11:23,

" *Truly I tell you, if anyone says to this mountain, Go, throw yourself into the sea, and does not doubt in their heart but believes that what they say will happen, it will be done for them.* "

The principal element in any magick is simply faith. We must believe that what we send out will not return to us void, but will indeed take place just as intended. Doubt, is the number one quenching factor that can snuff out the energy of magick and leave us feeling empty and powerless.

Many say that faith is the belief in things we cannot see. Yet if we train ourselves to be open to the things that are behind the common veil, we will

soon begin to see so much more than
the normal eye can see.

Let's use for example, the wind. We
can't necessary see the wind itself can
we? But, if we stop and look at the
trees and our surroundings we can see
the effect of the wind itself and thus
also can prove of its existence.

"Real change isn't accomplished by force, but it is accomplished more effectively by simply granting insight into the fault at hand."

Visualization & Circle Casting

In practicing any type of magick in a ritual or ceremony it is most common for us to want to prepare the area first. Casting a circle isn't mandatory in all circumstances however. Using Visualization skills and silent prayer/spell casting can be done from a distance, with no need of tools at all, for a knowledgeable and seasoned practitioner. I will go into this more at a later time.

In Kingdom magick, we use this practice called visualization to a great degree. We use it along some fundamental tools that help develop our direction of will and focus.

Visualization is simply the art of projecting our mental images, or our directed will, directly into our physical and/or spiritual world. We are seeing in our minds, the things we want to take place and thru visualization, we project that into the real world. What we must remember, is that in doing this, we are truly bringing into real action what is our will within us.

To visualize something happening is relatively simple isn't it? It is conquering our own self-doubt, and getting past heckles of the skeptic, that is the real chore. We must focus on our intent and be diligent in doing so. We must push past the normal walls found within the modern religious box, and grasp firmly to the belief and understanding that there is indeed, a real spark within us that is ready to burst into flames of real manifested power. This power can, and will change things.

Results may not be visually seen each time you try, but each time you try, it will become easier and more productive. Don't feel let down if your first results feel like, no results at all. I assure you, things did happen. In Visualization we don't always see external changes. For instance, I have used visualization in church to project healing in a sick individual. I would visualize the healing flowing through the sick person as a bright light, and then I would see the sickness leaving their bodies. At that particular time, the healing wasn't always noticed, but most often after only a few days, the individual would testify of their healing. Some changes are inward and may take some time for proof to be shown that it worked.

Using visualizing in the casting of a circle is simply projecting a protective barrier around us, or around our group. It is vital that we do so if we need to create what is called our sacred space. Casting a circle keeps out unwanted influences, and allows us to more effectively and safely, project our intent or prayer without negative energies hindering us. Our circle will be used to contain the positive energies that are raised and to harness them to their fullest.

Along with visualization, Kingdom
magick often utilizes the following tools:

1.) *Salt*
2.) *Incense or Candles*
3.) *Water (many prefer rain water)*
4.) *Wand or Athame*

Each of these tools represents a
different element. The elements are of
course what make up all that we see
physically around us. Here is each tool
and their associated element as it
applies to Kingdom magick.

1.) *Salt = The earth element*
2.) *Incense or Candle = the element of
fire.*
3.) *Water = The element of water*
4.) *Wand or Athame = the element of
air.*

Note: A few of the tools listed may be
used differently to some degree. The
Athame for example is at times used to
represent the element of fire in some

groups. If a person chooses to apply this to their individual practice, they simply need to remember to replace their element of air with a new applicable tool.

So, now we need to learn just how to cast our circle, don't we? We know the basic principles of visualization and a little about the tools we are going to use, but how do we actually do it? Be patient, were going to get to that, in just a second.

In Kingdom Magick we call in what is the four corners. Better said, we are going to call in the Guardians (also called the watchers) of those four corners. We do this to help us, and to protect us as we work to enter the spiritual world, and to bring about change in our sacred space. We do this, along with our visualization of course.

The four corners are simply the four corners of our Earth. They are as such,

1.) East
2.) South
3.) West
4.) North

In Kingdom Magick, It is preferred to move in a clock wise (To the right) formation while casting a circle. I personally like to begin with the eastern corner.

Now, before we start casting our first circle we need to examine and learn of the guardians or the watchers that watch over these four corners of the Earth, and their names. If you have studied other forms of magickal practices you may have heard of other titles or names other than the ones used in Kingdom magick. This is often done, and is based upon the individual practice and personal leading. In Kingdom Magick however, we use the four guardians and their names are as follows.

1.)Gabriel
2.)Uriel
3.)Michael
4.)Raphael

 These guardians or watchers as many know are of course, angels. They are spoken of in scriptures, and in many religious texts throughout the world. They are identified and spoken of in many different faiths, not just Christianity. The terminology may be slightly different but the experiences and encounters all point to the same conclusion. That conclusion is the reality of these messengers and helpers of humanity in all societies and traditions.

 Each guardians stands watch at a different corner of the Earth (thus the reason for the term watcher) ,and has authority over the wind of another direction. Each watcher or angel also represents an aspect of the elements.

1.)*Gabriel = Represents water (Tool=*

Water)
2.)<u>*Uriel*</u> *= Represents Earth (Tool= Salt)*

3.)<u>*Michael*</u> *= Represents Fire(Tool=*
Incense)

4.)<u>*Raphael*</u> *= Represents Air (Tool=*
wand or Athame)

Let's look at which corner is associated with each guardian or angel. They are as follows.

1.)<u>*Gabriel*</u> = Watcher over the West corner and angel of the north wind and the midnight wind.

2.)<u>*Uriel*</u> = Watcher over the North corner and angel of the South wind and the noonday wind.

3.) <u>*Michael*</u> *= Watcher over the South Corner and angel of the east wind and morning wind.*

4.)<u>*Raphael*</u> = Watcher over the East

corner and angel over the west wind and evening wind.

Before we move on let's look at a few Biblical scriptures, that speak of the corners and of the four angels.

1.)*Ezekiel 7:2* (Old Testament*)*

"The end! The end has come upon the four corners of the land." (NIV)

2.)*Isaiah 11:12* (Old Testament*)*

"He will raise a banner for the nations and gather the exiles of Israel; he will assemble the scattered people of Judah from the four quarters of the earth. (NIV)

3.)*Revelation 7:1* (New Testament*)*

"After this, I saw four angels standing at the four corners of the earth, holding back the four winds to prevent any wind from blowing on the land or on the sea or on any tree." (NIV)

There are many books out today that are free and great for researching. I urge each person to use what's readily available.

Future books on Kingdom Magick will dive deeper into the subject of the four corners and of the angels. It will also dive deeper into the art of casting our circles, and be full of Kingdom magick spells and prayers written by the Elijah Autumn. Remember in Kingdom magick, prayer and spell casting are somewhat the same.

A prayer can be seen as asking for direct divine intervention, while a spell is performing the task ourselves. Both can be done while in a sacred space. Just always remember, if the spirit leads us to perform the task ourselves, it will never oppose the direct free will of an individual. The only time that may not apply, might be in a protection spell or prayer. It is done so with permission of the one we are protecting, and done in a way that as long as the one attacking does not attack, there is no harm done.

In casting our circle each person may wish to alter their method slightly to fit their own personal preferences but here is a very basic method of casting a beginner circle. Kingdom magick volume two will be more in depth and filled with many spells from the author's book of shadows.

1.Choose a place where you have quiet. A place where you will not be interrupted. Try to find a place that has enough room for you and any tools you will be using.

2.Take a moment and clear your mind and begin focusing on your intent. Perhaps play some soft music and dim the lights?

3.Have your tools easily available to you and within reach.

4.*Will know and understand that each of our tools represents an element of the Mother Nature. With this said we will begin placing our symbolic tools at the designated locations.*

5.Starting from the East as described earlier, we will begin with Raphael, and using our wand or our Athame. Place in your right hand or whichever is your main writing hand your tool for the element of air. Moving in a clockwise rotation, visualize with you wand or Athame a protective barrier of light all around your scared space. Ask the Guardian to watch over you and to protect you as you move around your circle. Remember to place your tool at it appropriate place when you complete the circle. Example:

… Watcher and Guardian over the East and of the power of air … Raphael we ask of your time and your power. Assistant me/us, in my/our magickal workings. Grant me/us, protection and guidance. Raphael …I/we invoke thee.

6.Now move to the south and do much like the same thing but changing to the Guardian of the south which is Michael, and to the element of fire. Use the incense that you brought to the circle, and light it to represent the element of fire. Remember to move in a clockwise rotation with the incense and speak just as you did before. Remember to place your tool at it appropriate place when you complete the circle. Example:

...Watcher and Guardian over the South and of the power of fire ... Michael we ask of your time and your power. Assistant me/us, in my/our magickal workings. Grant me/us protection and guidance. Michael ... I/we invoke thee.

7.Now move to the western corner of your circle and proceed in the same way, but using the guardian of the west and its appropriate element. The watcher and guardian is Gabriel and the tool is of course water. Moving again in a clockwise rotation speak the words and sprinkle water around your circle. Remember to place your tool at it appropriate place when you complete the circle

…Watcher and Guardian over the West and of the power of water … Gabriel, we ask of your time, and your power. Assistant me/us, in my/our magickal workings. Grant me/us protection and guidance. Gabriel… I/we invoke thee.

1.) Finishing our circle, we end with the North. Uriel is our watcher and Guardian of the North. Our tool and element is salt. Complete the circle casting by moving again in a clockwise rotation. Sprinkle the salt around the circle and place the left over salt at the northern location. Remember to speak the words while you move. Example:

…Watcher and Guardian over the North and of the power of Earth …Uriel we ask of your time and your power.

Assistant me/us, in my/our magickal workings. Grant me/us protection and guidance. Uriel… I/we invoke thee.

Making sure we have placed each tool and element each of our four corners we can begin our magickal workings. Our circle is cast.

<u>Stay updated on Kingdom Magick Vol. 2 coming out in November!</u>

Reflections of the Divine

A sneak peek, at Elijah Autumns new book of articles, and topic ideas for group discussions.

Coming out in November 2013!

<u>Understanding Truth</u>

In a world of religions and mixed theologies, it can be so hard to find our way to a truth that is undeniable. It seems in every religion there are mixed and conflicting thoughts and ideas. There is rebellion and spiritual division. There is anger and bigotry in what should be houses of unconditional love. There are those who hold on to laws that no man can walk, and there are those that hold to no law or standard at all. What is the undeniable truth? Is it found in one faith or in one denomination? Is it discovered within ourselves or in others? Truth is a word that all mankind shouts it desires, yet it is truth that most men fear, and move to hide it under cover to avoid both ridicule and persecution.

People throughout our communities and nation walk every day to building seeking a truth that most often leaves them as empty when they leave as when they first arrived. Why is it that the hunger for spiritual truth seems only to grow in what should be a buffet of gourmet doctrines? The truth is simply that truth cannot complete us unless it is the complete truth. Just because the words we read are truth, means nothing if they are only a fragment of the whole truth. That would like offering a child half a puzzle and asking them to put it together and be happy with it.

I am no master of theology, and I am most definitely not a stranger to sin. Yet I know the truth, for it is truth that has set me free. What is that truth you ask? The truth is found within you my friend. It lies within us all when we are born. Jesus said that the Kingdom of God is within us. It is not outward and not around us, but within us. God is a spirit and the power and strength of all that is divine dwells within this Kingdom Jesus spoke of.

In 1 Corinthians 4:20 we read, "For the kingdom of God is not a matter of talk but of power." Do you have power in your faith? Do you see power in others in your faith? Perhaps this is why many of us feel incomplete? In our spirit, we know what Jesus told us don't we? We know of the miracles that not only Jesus preformed, but we also know of all the prophets of the Old Testament and the magnificent manifested power that they possessed in their lives.

The word spiritual power scares people doesn't it? It scared people even in Jesus's day. The religious leaders of the time killed him for it didn't they? Yet now, they worship him. Do you desire to live a life like Jesus did? Are you afraid to possess the same power that he held? I hope your answer is yes, you want to live as Jesus and no you are not afraid. If this is the case then you are close to being ready.

To understand truth for what it is, we must empty ourselves of preconceived ideas and thoughts. We must be open to the spirit, and if you are unlearned on spirit, stop and ask for wisdom from God right now. Despite what others will tell you, do not fear to walk into the unknown. Search out God and all that is divine. Read every book you can get and every letter or parcel the spirit tries to teach through. Stop and listen to the gentle voice that rides on the winds. Take a good hard look at the magnificent glory of creation and how life has continued throughout the years. Look within yourself and understand who it is that you are. You are child of God my friend.

Don't be afraid, but just believe. Follow the soft voice that lies within you that beckons you to love, and to try to learn everything you can. Real truth comes from spiritual revelation and not man. Yes, listen and respect those that seek to teach of God, but never stop seeking on your own and never let them limit your knowledge out of fear.

2.) **Undeniable Truth**

Undeniable truth rides on the whispering winds and it echoes off nature's magnificent beauty. Can you relate to what I just said? Understanding this statement requires a real spiritual connection with all that is God's. It means that we truly understand that there is more to this life than what we simply see with our physical eyes. God is a spirit, and the kingdom of God is within us. His spirit lives and breathes in everything that holds life. In such life, shines the face of a creator, so many, claim to never see. The minds and bodies of so many people are seen running to and fro. Running after something preconceived and programmed into their minds as what God should look like and then deny the spirit they seek repeatedly with no knowledge of whom they even were in contact with or had even seen.

So many want to fight what they don't understand but truth doesn't hide its face from us; it is us that refuse to see it. Since God is a spirit, to have a connection with the Divine requires us to understand spirituality. This is where many of our modern day churches have failed in their teaching of Christianity. I need to say that is. There is so much more to Christianity than what ninety percent of what most churches will ever teach. To be a Christian means we choose to follow Jesus but to do that, we have to understand all that he was, and is. Jesus preformed miracle after miracle. Let me pose this question that I know will stir the masses. Was Jesus's ability to perform miracles strictly because of his divinity, or was it because he simply understood who he was as God's child, just as all of us are? If the kingdom of God is within us, than can we do as Jesus said years ago, and do greater things than even he did in his life? Within each of us, the word of God says lays this kingdom of God, and thus all the powers of miracles lay as well.

Throughout history miracles and magick have been documented as real. The prophets of the Old Testament and religious figures all over the globe are witnessed to have performed such events and practices. Both good and bad people have been reported to have possessed such spiritual strength or power. To understand this all that is needed is for one to read their Bible. If this is the cause then where does such power come from? Many believe its God or Satan that grants such strength. But what if such power is universal, meaning, it is already a part of who we are as children of God and we all possess it regardless of how dormant it is or asleep. It is neither good nor bad but only becomes such out of the evil intentions or out of the corruption of a man's heart.

This is the meat of the matter then isn't it? Who are you and what lies within you? We live in a spiritual world even though many fail to see it, and there are many voices that can lead a man astray. Negative voices bring about discord and hate while those of a positive nature, bring about love and peace. Condemnation and hate were nowhere in the spirit of Christ and have no place in a Christian neither. Not a real one anyhow. To be a follower and disciple of Christ we walk according to his spirit. We believe the words he said and make every effort to install them into our daily lives.

We are in a spiritual war for there is evil in this world and in the spiritual realm. This evil doesn't want you to come to a realization of truth and who you are as a child of God. For you to understand the power within you to have victory over everything in your life would be a real problem for those seeking to control you wouldn't it? For this reason we must be willing to have ears for the spirit and to hear the voices that ride on the winds. Are you ready?

3.) Understanding ourselves

Understanding our own nature, and
who we are as individuals, can be a
task not many of us ever fully complete.
No matter our theology, the same
questions of self-meaning and purpose
fill our nights with spiritual explorations
and a quest to find each of our own
answers. Wisdom from the Heavens
and real revelation are called upon
when questions run so deep within all
of us.

The answers could be said to lie in
faith and trust. We need faith to help us
believe in something that though we
may not fully understand, regardless,
we will still stand upon its existence.
We need trust to believe that this divine
power will not lead us wrong, but will
only lead us into truth. It is complete
childlike submission to an inner voice

that calls out to us from a place so many never acknowledge, and thus never find the answers that burned within them. This place is the real Kingdom of God.

Becoming who our destiny calls us to be doesn't come from human will power; it comes from real divine intervention. We are born flawed and lacking of the wisdom and understanding of the hidden mysteries. They are hidden for a reason, and without a seeking spirit such wisdom and knowledge cannot be gained, for it is only for those willing to search. For this reason the Holy Bible tells us to seek the truth, and not to simply except any doctrine thrown our way.

Doctrines and theologies fill our country like a mangled mess of heresy and human ignorance. What brings about such confusion and multiple doctrines even in Christ's church? The answer is that people lacking in real revelation and those that have never had a divine encounter create doctrines created by their own traditions and imaginations. Many of these people were held high in the communities and thus they were trusted and followed. For this reason the Holy Bible says to measure what you hear.

 Our destiny is not found in fighting who we are, but it's found in simply surrendering to it. Laying our burdens and guilt's before a righteous God and allowing the direct hand of the divine to mold us as it is fit for us. No human strength except that of submission is required to become all we are intended to be. Know who you are and except it good or bad. Cry out to the Heavens for his mercy and guidance and a chain reaction of life experiences will take place that will be set to train you and prepare you. Acknowledge that all experiences work for the better good in all of us, even the painful ones.

 Wisdom does come with a price, yet without it, life is so incomplete. The price is paid by overcoming trials in your life and learning from them. The Bible says with wisdom comes much sorrow. Because when you finally see the truth of things your eyes will become open to such a torn world of spiritual chaos and division. There are no new revelations, for truth has always been the same, but there are new revelations in each of us as individuals and they come as the divine's hand sways in the wind.

 All of us are equal in the divine's eyes, no matter our theologies or our mistakes. Let no one criticize another for their place on the journey of life, for all of us are truth seekers, in hunt for our own answers. Instead, let us walk with each other and learn from each other. Just as the seekers of the old wrote down their revelations and spiritual encounters let us also consider doing the same for those that come after us. Let us stop the circle of division and chaos and reach out our hands of peace. Let each one of us search out our own salvation with fear and trembling before a Divine God, but may we shelter our brothers and sisters under the wings of his mighty angels and the love of mankind.

4.) <u>Don't limit yourself</u>

Born into a world of chaos and uncertainty, we struggle to find some kind of solid truth, in a mixing bowl of blended theories and confusing religious ideas. With all the different religions and faiths in our world it can be anything but easy to simply except what comes our way and preached to us, by any person claiming, to understand the truth and the hidden mysteries of the world.

There is truth and then there is complete truth. Many theories can indeed hold some fragments of solid truths to them but they limit their converts by not teaching all that makes up the essence of the whole picture of truth itself. Where do we find truth? Where do we find the answers that make up the universe? Do you want to find them?

  The Bible tells us to seek the truth. To truly seek truth however, I ask this. Can we limit ourselves to limited knowledge or should we dive into all the world has to offer? What I mean is this. The Bible contains only the letters and words chosen by the council to make up what is the main study guild of the Christian faith. The question is, were there others written and if so, why are they hidden? Could, only reading the 66 books in our Bibles limit our ability to completely grasp the complete truth of all things? Could that hinder Christ's people by removing certain fragments of what makes up all the pieces of this scattered jigsaw puzzle?

  The books in our Bible give us a basic blueprint of how to interpret truth and how to spot false ones but if there is more, should we not want to explore it and understand it. How many letters written to to the people are now hidden on the shelves of people that wish to put a limit on their readership? Why would anyone want to limit knowledge unless it was contain them or hinder them powerless?

I use Enoch as an example. Our Holy Bible tells us in Genesis 5:24 that "Enoch walked faithfully with God; then he was no more, because God took him away". Now I ask this question, why were the books of Enoch removed from most Holy Bibles in our country, if he indeed did walk with God? Wouldn't a person desiring a walk with God want to read everything about a man that truly did?

I will lend this column with this note, and let this be part one of many to come. Read your Bible and all the words within it. Then use that knowledge to advance your knowledge and spiritual maturity by reaching outside the walls of corporate religion. Take the hand of Christ and let him show you all That God was, and is, and is to come.

5.)Finding the answers

Questions about life, love and God are probably seen today as the three most complex questions, any person could ever ask. But are they truly so complex? Have we as a people simply made them complex by looking too deep into something that in reality is not so difficult at all? Can we often alter or create difficulties in the simple things, due to our need to rationalize everything with human logic? Could part of the problem be our inability to simply accept the things we cannot change? Could in fact we say that often it is our own personal desires to mold things in what would be our best selfish interest, that actually deters us from receiving what it is that we are even after in the first place. I believe so.

All of us come from different walks of life and traditions. We were all raised slightly different. Our understandings of things may be seen differently and our perceptions of how things should work are often not on the same side of the scale as others. This can cause wrongful judging, due to many times the judgment is solely based on outside appearance rather than a firsthand knowledge of the truth. In order to understand why it is we do things, or why others have done things we must understand the differences between how we were raised and the concept of simple truth. Meaning just because we were raised to believe one thing, doesn't mean that one thing is truth, but may be simply tradition.

Truth is what it is. No matter the perception, it does not change. It is that truth though that finds it so hard to reach the human heart, for we are a strong and opinionated people. Things like love and the purpose of life burn in the hearts of most mankind. People run about in search of the answers based upon what they were taught they should be, but are they searching for what they really are? Do we often find the truth and yet deny it, because we never saw it standing right in front of us, because it wasn't what we thought it should be? Yes, I believe we often do.

Is love so hard to understand? How can something that happens so naturally be so difficult to comprehend? Is it that we try to justify everything and use logic in matters of the heart when love is anything but logical? If God is love as the Bible says, can we really understand it if we don't know God personally? Perhaps our inability to figure out love is in the fact that love is the essence of God within us and to tap into it, we need to know the answers to all three of these questions of life, love and God?

Is the purpose of life to love, to discover love and to learn to love? To worship God requires love does it not?

Can all the answers we seek in life all revolve around the one emotion that we call love? That is why we find so many lost and confused people in the world. They have filled themselves with so much hate that love has no room to grow or teach, and they die in their own black hearts and unanswered questions. In this world men find it so hard to express love due to traditions or peer pressure. Many go about screaming inwardly yet stay silent in their own desires, and I ask - why? Love is natural and we should not fight it. To love is to live, and a life without love, is no real life at all.

The answers are simple. But they are not found in the normal human search. The answers are found within you and not around you. The kingdom that holds the answers is within and unless we are willing to silence the chaos and listen, our chances of finding truth is bleak. The world is full of madness and a disregard for the things of God. Love cannot be found in worldly things because God is love - remember that. God is not about churches, temples or synagogues; he is about love, creation, and order.

Love is not just for the soft but for all of us as God's creation. Every man and woman on earth is entitled to it. It is a free gift of God and most certainly a powerful one.

Watch for 'Reflections of the Divine', in your local bookstores and online!

* 9 7 8 0 6 1 5 8 8 8 0 5 7 *